Green Church

Leader Guide

Also available

Green Church:
Reduce, Reuse,
Recycle, Rejoice!
Book

Burst:
Green Church
A Study for Youth

Green Church:
Caretakers of
God's Creation
A Study for Children

7 Simple Steps
to Green Your Church
A Handbook for Everyone

Green Church

REDUCE, REUSE, RECYCLE, REJOICE!

Leader Guide

Pamela Dilmore
and Rebekah Simon-Peter

Abingdon Press
Nashville

GREEN CHURCH
REDUCE, REUSE, RECYCLE, REJOICE!
LEADER GUIDE
by Pamela Dilmore
and Rebekah Simon-Peter

ISBN 978-1-426-70294-5

FSC
Mixed Sources
Product group from well-managed
forests, controlled sources and
recycled wood or fiber
Cert no. SCS-COC-002464
www.fsc.org
©1996 Forest Stewardship Council

10 11 12 13 14 15 16 17 18 19—10 9 8 7 6 5 4 3 2

Manufactured in the United States of America.

Contents

Introduction

Christians hear about global warming and damage to God's creation. They want to help, but how? This leader guide will help you and your congregation explore this critically important topic from a Christian perspective with a six-week, small-group study using the book *Green Church: Reduce, Reuse, Recycle, Rejoice!* written by Rebekah Simon-Peter.

Using Scripture and scientific findings, the study will look at God's Word, God's world, and our response. The journey begins where we are and helps us think through what we know, what we can learn, and what we can do to make a difference. Through the study, we will learn that we can do many things, small and large, that will help to heal God's world.

Resources for a Green Church small-group study include the book *Green Church*; this easy-to-use leader guide, with step-by-step instructions for leading your group; an optional companion book called *7 Simple Steps to Green Your Church*; and Web support at *greenchurch.cokesbury.com* with a variety of tools that can be used in your group. These resources are described below.

You may also want to consider expanding your Green Church study to include the entire congregation, using the youth study *Burst: Green Church* and the children's study *Green Church: Caretakers of God's Creation*. Each of these parallel studies is six weeks long, enabling you to create a church-wide program for all age levels. You will find a plan for doing so in the section of this leader guide called "Organizing a Church-wide Program."

Green Church: Reduce, Reuse, Recycle, Rejoice!

This book by Rebekah Simon-Peter, on which the study is based, contains six thought-provoking chapters. These chapters provide the basis for the small-group sessions. The book can also be used for individual study or as a study book for a Green Church retreat.

For small-group use, you will begin with a key Scripture and a question that will help you engage the main focus for the chapter. You will explore the question by reflecting upon and discussing relevant portions of God's Word and scientific information about God's world. This parallel focus on Scripture and science will help you glimpse God's vision for the good of all creation and ponder ways in which we have strayed from that vision.

Chapter format will help you to identify ways you can respond to what you have learned and participate in healing God's world. Helpful sidebars include "Question," "Spotlight on Science," and "Green Fact." Each chapter offers additional activity suggestions in "Greening the Church." Chapter titles are:

1. Repent

2. Reclaim

3. Reduce

4. Reuse

5. Recycle

6. Rejoice!

Green Church Leader Guide

This leader guide provides everything you need to organize, facilitate, and lead a Green Church small-group study. Easy-to-use instructions will help you publicize the study and recruit participants. Tips are included for leading the group in a way that will encourage discussion and a sense of community and friendship, creating an atmosphere of respect and commitment among the group members. Detailed session plans for each of the chapters will help you prepare for the sessions and lead them with confidence. The session plans will include Bible study, discussion and reflection, individual and group activities, prayers, and follow-up suggestions.

Using this leader guide, you will be able to help your group experience a sense of community, feel comfortable about sharing their opinions and ideas, learn what the Bible and scientific research tell us about our world, and identify what to do in order to be better stewards of God's creation

7 Simple Steps to Green Your Church

The companion book, *7 Simple Steps to Green Your Church,* by Rebekah Simon-Peter, can be used as part of the study or as a stand-alone tool. It is a step-by-step guide to greening your church over the course of one year, from forming a team to calculating the church's carbon footprint to paying it forward with another congregation. Each month during the year focuses on a different area, such as "The Resurrected Life: Recycling," "Let There Be Light: Lighting," and "To Everything There Is a Season: Heating and Cooling."

Part One

Getting Organized

Starting a
Green Church Group

A well-known line from the movie *Field of Dreams* promises the lead character, Ray Kinsella, "If you build it, they will come." He responds by building a baseball diamond in his cornfield. Some old-time baseball players, including Kinsella's father, come and play in the field, showing the promise to be true.

The promise might also be applied to organizing and starting small-group studies in the church. However, starting or "building" a small-group study means more than simply announcing it and waiting for participants to show up. Building a group is not difficult, but it takes time and planning. Follow these easy steps to get your group going.

Choose a Meaningful Topic

You have already taken this first important step. *Green Church: Reduce, Reuse, Recycle, Rejoice!* addresses an issue of great concern in our world. As Christians, we want to know how to honor God's creation and how to repair harm we may have done to our environment.

Become Familiar With the Study Content

Read through *Green Church: Reduce, Reuse, Recycle, Rejoice!* Study the related Bible readings mentioned in the chapters. Look at the suggested websites. Think about the topic and the issues it generates. Consider the biblical vision as it relates to care of our world. Prepare to respond to questions.

Develop a List of Potential Participants

An ideal size for a small group is 7 to 12 people. Your list should have about twice your target number (perhaps 14–24 people). Encourage your church to purchase a copy of the book for each person on your list. Besides encouraging the involvement of church members, this effort can be a way of reaching out to those who may not be actively involved in your church.

Decide on a Place and Time for Your Group Meeting

Take into account how much time you have available for each session and how much you want to cover in each of the meetings. (See the sections in this book called "Choosing Study Options" and "Organizing a Church-wide Program." Consider which of these options, or others you may think of, might work best in your church.

Contact Potential Participants

Identify someone who is willing to go with you to visit the people on your list. Call or e-mail the people on your list; and set up a time for a brief visit with them, if possible. Make it your goal to become acquainted with each person you visit. Tell them about the Green Church study, including time, place, and number of weeks the group will meet. Invite them to become part of the group. Thank them for their time. Then give them a copy of the book. Even if they choose not to attend the group, they will have an opportunity to read the book on their own.

Advertise the Study

Publicize the study through as many channels as are available in your church and your community. You will probably find that people who are not on your original list or even in your church will be interested in the study and want to attend.

Remind Participants

A few days before the sessions begin, make friendly phone calls or send e-mails to thank all persons you visited as well as others who may have registered to attend the study for their consideration and interest. Remind them of the time and location of the first meeting. Include directions to the meeting place.

.

Leading a Green Church Group

The thought of leading a small group can be intimidating. You probably have many questions. How much work will be required of me? Do I have to be an expert on environmental issues? What must I do to make the small-group experience meaningful?

A small-group leader does not have to be an expert. In fact, a leader often learns along with the participants in the group. The role of a leader is to prepare for and facilitate the group sessions in order to help people explore, engage, reflect upon, discuss, and apply the material to their daily lives. The leader and participants will study and learn together. So, what does a Green Church leader actually do?

A Leader Prepares

This leader guide contains instructions for planning and implementing a study based on the book *Green Church: Reduce, Reuse, Recycle, Rejoice!* by Rebekah Simon-Peter. The guide includes session plans for each chapter of the book. However, there are also things you will want to do every week to prepare, no matter what the session topic is.

Pray. Ask for God's guidance as you prepare to lead the sessions.

Read and reflect. Before the session, review the chapter as well as the Bible readings, websites, and other sources mentioned.

Make notes about what you read. Jot down any questions or insights that occur to you during your reading.

Think about the participants. Who are the people who have decided to be part of your Green Church group? What life issues do they have? What questions might they have about the chapter that will be explored in the session? What questions might they have about the Bible readings associated with the chapter?

Gather supplies. Collect any needed supplies, such as nametags, large sheets of paper, markers, masking tape, writing paper, pencils, Bibles, and any audiovisual equipment you might need. As an additional option, you may want to consider bringing a computer and an LCD projector to the room if this equipment is available in your church. The group might enjoy looking at some of the websites mentioned in the chapters.

Prepare the learning area. Make sure everyone will have a comfortable place to sit. If the participants will write or do other activities during the session, make sure to have a table in the learning area. Some adults in your group may have difficulty standing or moving about. Take their needs into account. Will the learning area be suitable for activities in which the participants will get out of their chairs or use markers, paper, scissors, glue, and other art media? Can you easily use audiovisual equipment if you have this option? Where are the electrical outlets? Where will you project images? Will you need a screen, or can you use a wall? Will everyone be able to see what you project?

Pray for group participants. Before participants arrive, pray for each one. Ask for God's blessing on your session. Offer thanks for the opportunity to lead the session and to become better acquainted with all the participants.

A Leader Creates a Welcoming Atmosphere

Hospitality is a spiritual discipline. A small-group leader helps to create an environment that makes everyone feel welcome and helps every participant experience the freedom to ask questions and to state opinions. Such an atmosphere is based upon mutual respect. People have different ideas and points of view about most topics.

Issues related to the environment and global warming frequently generate opposing points of view. This Green Church study attempts to move beyond such differences. It is designed to explore the core biblical values related to caring for God's creation and to encourage stewardship of God's world. As Rebekah Simon-Peter writes in her introduction, "This study . . . aims to help you think and act communally for the good of God's creation."

At the beginning of the study, tell participants that they probably have different ideas and opinions about threats to our environment. Remind everyone to listen to and respect what others in the group might have to say, even when they disagree. Use the following three practices to nurture and model hospitality in your group:

Greet participants as they arrive. If you do not know the person, introduce yourself and ask for his or her name. As you greet each participant, say aloud his or her name. Invite everyone to wear nametags.

Listen. As the group discussion unfolds, listen to the comments and ideas of participants. Avoid the temptation to dominate conversation or "correct" the ideas of the participants. Your ability to listen is essential in creating and nurturing an atmosphere of trust and respect.

Affirm. Closely related to listening is affirming the ideas and opinions of the participants. Tell participants that you hear and understand what they are saying. If you do not understand, ask for clarification or further explanation. Thank them for telling about what they think or feel. Acknowledge their contributions in positive ways even if you disagree with their ideas. Affirming everyone's contribution will help to create trust and respect within your group.

A Leader Facilitates Discussion

Starting and keeping a discussion going is not as difficult as you might think. Most adults are willing to express their point of view even if they have a more introspective nature. The Green Church study deals with issues and actions related to the environment and global warming, topics about which people may have strong opinions, so you will probably have little difficulty starting a discussion. Your role will more likely involve helping the participants listen to one another and respect one another's point of view. With this aim in mind, the following steps will help you facilitate meaningful discussion:

Ask questions. Use the questions suggested in the session plans or other questions that occur to you as you prepare for the session. Encourage others to ask questions.

Invite silent participants to contribute ideas. If someone in the group is quiet, you might say, "I'm interested in what you're thinking." If participants seem hesitant or shy, do not pressure them to speak. However, do communicate your interest. Most of the time, you will discover that the quiet person has interesting ideas and will tell the group about them. Some people need an invitation in order to feel comfortable about discussing their ideas in a group.

Gently redirect discussion when someone in the group dominates. You can redirect discussion in several ways. Remind the group that everyone's ideas are important. Invite them to respect one another and to allow others in the group to express their ideas. You may establish a group covenant that clarifies such mutual respect. Such a covenant works best when the participants offer the terms upon which they will all agree. Taking time at the beginning of your group experience to establish such a covenant will help you if someone has a tendency to dominate.

Another tool is to use a structured group discussion activity such as allowing everyone a chance to speak for a specified amount of time. A typical way to begin this type of discussion is to say, "We will go around the circle, and each person will have thirty seconds to tell what they feel or think about this topic. Each person may either speak or pass. We will begin with the person on my right and continue until everyone has had a chance to speak."

Only as a last resort, take a moment after the session to speak to a person who dominates conversation. Do not embarrass the person in front of the other group participants.

Choosing Study Options

The Green Church study is suitable for use in a variety of Christian education settings. In order to choose the best option for your group, you will need to think about the amount of time you have, the locations available, and the ways in which the study might work best in your church.

Weeknight Small Group

A small-group study on a weeknight offers the best opportunity for doing the study in six sessions. Such small groups work well with a session that lasts an hour and a half. This length of time will provide excellent opportunities for reflection and discussion.

Sunday School

While Sunday school classes generally last for one hour, people like to enjoy a time of visiting when they arrive. Realistically, you may have 30 to 40 minutes for actual study. One way to cover the material and provide adequate time for group reflection and discussion is to do each chapter of the book for two Sundays. Thus, the study may be done for as long as 12 weeks. Adjust the time according to the needs of your group.

Weekend Retreat

A Green Church study works well as a weekend retreat. The following schedule shows how it might work for an all-day Saturday retreat.

8:00–8:30 A.M.	Arrival
8:30–10:00 A.M.	Chapter 1 session
10:00–10:30 A.M.	Break with refreshments
10:30 A.M.–Noon	Chapter 2 session
12:00–1:00 P.M.	Lunch
1:00–2:30 P.M.	Chapter 3 session
2:30–3:00 P.M.	Break with refreshments
3:00–4:30 P.M.	Chapter 4 session
4:30–5:00 P.M.	Free time
5:00–6:00 P.M.	Dinner
6:00–7:30 P.M.	Chapter 5 session
7:30–8:00 P.M.	Break with refreshments
8:00–9:30 P.M.	Chapter 6 session
9:30–9:45 P.M.	Closing devotion and dismissal

Organizing a Church-wide Program

All over the world people are becoming more concerned about energy use, climate change, endangered species, trash disposal, clean water, safe food, and other issues directly and indirectly related to care of the environment. Choosing to be good stewards of God's creation is deeply rooted and supported by the Bible. God created, loves, and sustains our world; and God calls us to love and care for all creation.

A church-wide Green Church study will give children, youth, and adults an opportunity to explore practical ways to respond to God's call to be good stewards. A church-wide program offers opportunities for learning, for intergenerational projects and activities, and for reaching out to the community through the programs and activities to address critical environmental concerns.

Resources for a Church-wide Study

Adults
- *Green Church: Reduce, Reuse, Recycle, Rejoice!*
  by Rebekah Simon-Peter
- *Green Church: Reduce, Reuse, Recycle, Rejoice! Leader Guide,*
  by Pamela Dilmore and Rebekah Simon-Peter

Youth
- *Burst: Green Church,* by Tim Gossett
- *Burst: Green Church Leader Guide,* by Tim Gossett

Children
- *Green Church: Caretakers of God's Creation,*
  by Suzann Wade and Daphna Flegal

Everyone
- *7 Simple Steps to Green Your Church,* by Rebekah Simon-Peter

Schedule for a Church-wide Study

Many churches have **weeknight programs** that include an evening meal; an intergenerational gathering time; and classes for children, youth, and adults. The following schedule illustrates one way to organize a weeknight program.

30 minutes	Gather for a meal
15 minutes	Intergenerational gathering that features a green topic. This may include audio-visual presentations, skits, music, fact presentations, and opening prayer related to good stewardship.
60 minutes	Classes for children, youth, and adults

Churches may want to do the study as a **Sunday school** program. This setting would be similar to the weeknight setting. The following schedule takes into account a shorter class time, which is the norm for Sunday morning programs.

10 minutes	Intergenerational gathering that features a green topic
30-40 minutes	Classes for children, youth, and adults

Choose a schedule that works best for your congregation and its existing Christian education programs. End your program with a church-wide celebration of your green study

Planning and Implementing Group Sessions

Before the first session, make sure everyone has a copy of *Green Church: Reduce, Reuse, Recycle, Rejoice!* and ask them to read the introduction and Chapter 1 ahead of time. Reading the material before the group meets each week will contribute to better discussion and learning in the group sessions.

As you lead your group in the study, you will move through a sequence of activities described in the paragraphs below. These activities are designed to bring the group together; to create a positive environment for learning and action; and to help the group engage the content, Bible readings, and other information provided in each book chapter. The goal is to help participants discover what the Bible and scientific research have to say about God's world and to help them identify ways they can be good stewards of that world. Such stewardship nurtures spiritual growth and commitment to Christian faith.

You will find step-by-step instructions for each session in Part Two: Session Plans. No matter what the topic, though, you will want to use the following process for each session:

Prepare. Before the session begins, review the chapter, the Bible readings, any websites you might choose to view, and the session plan. Gather supplies. Set up the learning area.

Welcome participants. Greet them as they arrive. Invite them to use nametags. When all group members are present, make sure they have a comfortable place to sit. Use this time to get acquainted or to catch up with one another and what has happened during the past week. Introduce any newcomers to the group.

Open the session. Introduce the session topic. Read the title, the Scripture, and the opening paragraph at the beginning of each chapter. Lead the group in the prayer provided with the session plan or in a prayer of your own.

Consider the question. Each chapter includes a box labeled "Question." This material is designed to stimulate reflection and discussion. It also provides a non-threatening way for participants to express their thoughts and feelings about the chapter topic.

Explore the chapter. Each chapter offers content based on biblical readings and scientific research. Guide your group through the highlights of this material, using the suggestions in the session plans. In each chapter you will find sidebars with additional information or activities. These sidebars are labeled "Spotlight on Science" and "Green Fact." We recommend that you start each session with the Scriptures noted. After you read the Scriptures, decide what you would like to discuss and in what order. You can adjust session plans to meet the needs, concerns, and ideas of your particular group.

Look ahead. Each chapter offers suggestions for things to do after the session in the sections entitled "Greening the Church" and "Follow Up." Invite participants to follow those suggestions in the week ahead. Encourage them to read the next chapter of the book and the Scriptures for that chapter. Invite them to note insights or questions they would like to talk about during the next session. The final session will include an opportunity for participants to discuss what they have learned and what difference their learning will make in their efforts to be good stewards of God's creation.

Close the session. Pray together using the prayer in the session plan or one of your own. If you use the prayers included in the session plans, you can read them aloud yourself, have a participant read them aloud, or make copies so that the group can pray aloud together.

Part Two

Session Plans

1. Repent

This session explores our need to repent for ways in which we have failed to be good stewards of God's creation.

Genesis 1:1–2:4; 6:1–9:17

Prepare

Read and review session materials.

- Pray for God's guidance as you read and think about the content for this session.
- Read Genesis 1:1–2:4; 6:1–9:17. Write notes about insights and questions that occur to you as you read.
- Read the Introduction and Chapter 1 in the book *Green Church: Reduce, Reuse, Recycle, Rejoice!* Make notes about insights or questions you have. Consider how your group might respond to the material. Write questions you think they might ask about the material.
- Review any websites you might want to show to the group.
- Review the Chapter 1 session plan.

Gather supplies.

- Bibles
- Additional copies of the book, if needed
- Nametags
- Large sheets of paper (preferably recycled) or a marker-board and markers
- Masking tape
- 8½" x 11" paper (preferably recycled)
- Pens or pencils
- Unscented candle and matches
- Used worship bulletins, one for each participant
- (Optional) Audiovisual equipment such as a computer and an LCD projector for viewing websites

Set up the learning area.

- Chairs. Make sure everyone will have a comfortable place to sit. Arrange chairs in a circle to promote group interaction.
- Table for supplies and a place to work. Participants may need to use a tabletop for writing or other creative activities. Make sure to consider the needs of those who have physical impairments.
- Small table for a worship center. Cover with an attractive cloth and place in the center of the room. Place the unscented candle and matches on the table.
- (Optional) Screen or wall to project websites using the LCD projector

Welcome Participants

- Arrive early. Pray for participants and for this Green Church session concerning our need to repent for ways in which we have failed to be good stewards of God's creation.
- Greet participants by name as they arrive. If you do not know them, introduce yourself and ask their names. Invite everyone to use nametags. Make sure everyone has a comfortable place to sit.
- Invite participants to introduce themselves and to tell everyone what brought them to the group. Ask: What excites you about this Green Church study?
- Give a copy of the book to anyone who does not yet have one.

Open the Session

- Invite participants to open their books and look at the layout of the chapters. Tell them that in each meeting, the group will read the Bible; consider a key question related to the session topic; review and discuss highlights of the chapter content and the information offered in the boxes labeled "Question," "Green Fact," and "Spotlight on Science." Then consider individual and group actions that could lead to better stewardship of God's creation. Point out each of the features in the boxes. Encourage participants to use the suggestions in "Greening the Church" between group meetings.

- Review highlights of the Introduction. Ask: What does "going green" mean to you? How do you see environmental stewardship as part of your life with God? How do you respond to the idea that humans have become "un-creators" of our earth? What feelings or thoughts do you have about acting communally for the good of God's creation?

- Invite someone to read aloud the chapter title, the opening Scripture (Genesis 1:31), and the quotation at the beginning of the chapter. Invite the group to spend a few moments in silent, prayerful reflection.

- Lead the group in this opening prayer: Creator God, reveal to us the ways in which we have sinned against you and your creation. Guide us in the way of repentance; in the name and spirit of Jesus, we pray. Amen.

Consider the Question

Read aloud the material from the participant's book entitled "Question." Ask participants to circle the number that best describes their answer. Invite them to tell how they answered and why.

Explore the Chapter
Read and discuss Genesis 1:1–2:4; 6:1–9:17.

Form two teams. Assign Genesis 1:1–2:4 and the section titled "The Days of Creation" to Team 1. Assign Genesis 6:1–7:24 and the sections "The Grief of God" and "The Process of

35

De-creation" to Team 2. Ask them in their team meetings to read or review highlights of their assigned Bible readings and chapter sections. Ask them to discuss the following questions: What do these Scriptures say to you about God's relationship to creation? about God's desire and intent for creation? What parts of the reading challenge or surprise you?

Bring the teams back together as one group. Tell them to give reports of their readings and discussions to the entire group. Ask: How do you respond to God's creation? to God's grief? to God's "de-creation"? What feelings or thoughts do you have about the relationship between these Scriptures and the issue of environmental stewardship?

Review highlights of Genesis 8:1–9:17 and the section "God Repented." Ask: What especially strikes you in this account of God's covenant with humankind and with all creation? What do you learn about God's faithfulness to the covenant? about our human faithfulness to the covenant? about our human need to repent?

Review and discuss "Ecological Meltdown."

Invite participants to spend a few moments reviewing the facts cited in "Ecological Meltdown." Ask them to note facts that surprise or disturb them. After a few moments, read aloud the following quotation from "God's Earth Is Sacred: An Open Letter to Church and Society in the United States," a statement from the National Council of Churches:

> God's creation delivers unsettling news. Earth's climate is warming to dangerous levels; 90 percent of the world's fisheries have been depleted; coastal development and pollution are causing a sharp decline in ocean health; shrinking habitat threatens to extinguish thousands of species; over 95 percent of the contiguous United States forests have been lost; and almost half of the population in the United States lives in areas that do not meet national air quality standards. . . . We have become un-Creators. Earth is in jeopardy at our hands.[1]

Ask the group to tell about unsettling news they have seen, experienced, or heard about in the natural world around them. List responses on a large sheet of paper or a markerboard for all to see. Ask: Which items are most distressing to you and why?

Review and discuss "Our Need to Repent."

Tell the group about the highlights or main points of this section. Ask: How do you respond to the author's recognition of her role in making a difference? Have you had similar feelings? If so, tell about them.

Invite participants to listen to and reflect on the following: Think about how you would feel if a favorite spot in nature were to disappear, if a favorite creature were to go extinct, or if a favorite season were to lose its distinctiveness? How might you respond?

Ask them to write or draw about their reflection on a sheet of paper. If any would like to talk about what they have written or drawn, allow them to do so. Do not pressure them to talk if they seem reluctant to do so. Read aloud the last two paragraphs of "Our Need to Repent."

Green Fact

Review the material in "Green Fact: Where's the Beef?" Calculate how much your group could reduce its carbon footprint by eating vegetarian one day a week for the duration of the study. If group members express interest, invite them to make a commitment to eat a vegetarian meal once a week during the study. Consider planning a "green" potluck for your group or the church.

Spotlight on Science

Read aloud the material in "Spotlight on Science: Figuring Environmental Impact." Ask: Do you agree or disagree? Why? Explain your response. How do you see the role of technology in relation to environmental stewardship?

Greening the Church

Read the material in "Greening the Church," and use it as an opportunity to consider whether your church might want to do as suggested. Distribute worship bulletins to participants. Tell them to mark anything that highlights the creation and our relationship to it. If possible, make a short visit to the sanctuary. Ask the group to describe elements of the sanctuary such as banners, wall hangings, stained-glass windows, or architectural features that highlight creation. Use the questions provided in "Greening the Church" to stimulate reflection and discussion.

Look Ahead

Encourage the group to read Chapter 2, "Reclaim," and the Bible readings (Genesis 1:26–3:21; Psalm 8:3-4) before the next session.

Invite participants to contact one another by phone or e-mail to offer mutual support for their efforts to be better stewards of creation.

Close the Session

Light a candle, and lead your group in a prayer of repentance. Ask group members to offer one-sentence prayers of repentance; then invite the group to respond, "O Creator, have mercy on us." You may also choose to use the responsive prayer included below. Pray aloud the lines shown in regular print, and invite the group to respond with the lines in bold.

We beg forgiveness for our blind focus
upon only one species, our own.
O Creator, have mercy on us.

For the times we have failed to think
of the harm done to other life.
O Creator, have mercy on us.

For our reckless plundering and waste
of so much that has value we do not yet perceive.
O Creator, have mercy on us.

We are children of God.
    We carry with us the promise that we are loved.
    Each day is new.
    The future is open.
Great Spirit, open our hearts.

> Donn Kesselheim
> Quaker Earthcare Witness
> Lander, Wyoming

[1]"The Earth Is Sacred: An Open Letter to Church and Society in the United States," The Nation Council of Churches (February 14, 2005).

2. Reclaim

This session explores how we can reclaim our God-given role as stewards of creation.

Genesis 1:26–3:21; Psalm 8:3-4

Prepare

Read and review session materials.
- Pray for God's guidance as you read and think about the content for this session.
- Read Genesis 1:26–3:21 and Psalm 8:3-4. Write notes about insights and questions that occur to you as you read.
- Read Chapter 2 in the book *Green Church: Reduce, Reuse, Recycle, Rejoice!* Make notes about insights or questions you have. Consider how your group might respond to the material. Write questions you think they might ask.
- (Optional) Review the websites for the National Audubon Society (*audubon.org*), the National Geographic Society (*news.nationalgeographic.com*), and NASA (*nasa.gov*). Consider showing these to the group to stimulate discussion.
- Review the Chapter 2 session plan.

Gather supplies.
- Bibles
- Additional copies of the book, if needed
- Nametags
- Large sheets of paper (preferably recycled) or a markerboard and markers
- Masking tape
- 8½" x 11" paper (preferably recycled)

- Pens or pencils
- Unscented candle and matches
- A dictionary
- (Optional) Audiovisual equipment such as a computer and an LCD projector for viewing websites

Set up the learning area.

- Chairs. Make sure everyone will have a comfortable place to sit. Arrange chairs in a circle to promote group interaction.
- Table for supplies and a place to work. Participants may need to use a tabletop for writing or other creative activities. Make sure to consider the needs of those who have physical impairments.
- Small table for a worship center. Cover with an attractive cloth. Place the unscented candle and matches on the table.
- (Optional) Screen or wall to project websites with the LCD projector
- If you decide to do a church tour during your meeting time as described in "Greening the Church," think about where you will go and what the group will look at. You may also choose to do this activity at another time, for example, immediately after the group meeting or during the week before the next session.
- If you decide to go outside during your meeting time, consider where you will go and how long you will be there.

Welcome Participants

- Arrive early. Pray for all the participants and for this Green Church session about reclaiming our role as God's stewards.
- Greet participants by name as they arrive. If you do not know them, introduce yourself and ask their names. Encourage everyone to wear nametags. Make sure everyone has a comfortable place to sit.

- Invite participants to tell about any insights they gained from doing the activities in the "Greening the Church" section.
- Give a copy of the book to anyone who does not have one.

Open the Session

- Invite someone to read aloud the title, the opening Scripture (Genesis 1:26), and the opening paragraph at the beginning of the chapter. Invite the group to spend a few moments in silent, prayerful reflection.
- Lead the group in this prayer: Generous and benevolent God, we thank you for creating us in your image. Help us to reclaim your image and likeness and to maintain the goodness, wholeness, and integrity of all that you have created; in the name and spirit of Jesus we pray. Amen.

Consider the Question

Read aloud the material in the box entitled "Question." Ask participants to circle the response that best describes their answer or to write a sentence that expresses what they believe. Invite them to tell how they answered and why.

Explore the Chapter

Read and discuss Psalm 8:3-8 and Genesis-charge.

Ask participants to find a partner. Invite them to read Psalm 8:3-8 and to take a couple of minutes to tell one another how they might answer the psalmist's question.

After two or three minutes, read aloud Psalm 8:3-8 from *The Message*. Ask: How do you respond to the term *Genesis-charge?* What does it say to you about God's expectations for us with regard to creation? Ask: How do you define *stewardship?* Write responses on a large sheet of paper or a markerboard for all to see.

Review highlights of the section titled "Stewardship." Ask: What connections do you see among Genesis-charge, stewardship, and Psalm 8:3-8?

43

Illustrate or write about Genesis 1:26.

Read aloud Genesis 1:26. Then read aloud the following paragraph from the participant's book titled "The Crown of Creation."

> Rather than the habitat itself giving rise to a new inhabitant, our template is divine. We alone are patterned after the Creator's own self. While the rest of creation bears the fingerprints of God, we bear the very stamp of God. Made in the image and likeness of God, humans are the crown of creation.

Ask: How do you respond to this paragraph? Invite participants to think about what it means to be made in the image of God. Give everyone paper and pens or pencils. Invite them to make a sketch or to write words that represent the image of God. Invite participants to tell about what they have sketched or written. Ask: Was this task easy or difficult for you? Why? What do you think it means to be created in the image of God?

Explore Genesis 2:4–3:21.

Form teams of two or three. Ask them to read Genesis 2:4–3:21 and the material related to this Scripture in the section called "The Crown of Creation." Ask them to identify what the humans gain from creation. Ask: In what ways does God support or provide for the humans through creation? After a few minutes, ask the teams to tell about one thing they identified. List their responses on a large sheet of paper or on a markerboard. Ask: What insights does this list offer about human dependency upon creation?

Reflect on meanings of "Deconstructing Dominion."

Read the opening paragraph in the section called "Deconstructing Dominion." Invite participants to tell how they define the word *dominion.* Ask a participant to locate the word in a dictionary and read aloud the definitions for this word.

Once again, read aloud Genesis 1:26. Review highlights of the section titled "Deconstructing Dominion." Ask: How does the information in this section affect your understanding of the word *dominion*? How do you think the word reflects human responsibility for creation? How do you respond to the insight that dominion offers humans the opportunity to "mirror God's self back to the creation"? What attributes does the author use to describe God in this section? How does she see humans reflecting the image of God through dominion over creation?

Discuss "Original Blessing."

Ask for a volunteer to read aloud Genesis 1:27-31. Ask: How do you see God's blessing in this Scripture? How do you see God's blessing in creation today? How do you think we can "reclaim" God's "original blessing" of creation?

Write "Subdue" on a large sheet of paper or on a markerboard. Ask: What words or phrases come to mind when you hear the word *subdue*? Write the group's responses on the paper or markerboard beneath the word.

Review highlights of the information about *subdue* in this section. Ask: How does this information change or influence your understanding of the word? Read aloud the last sentence in "Original Blessing": "If humans, fish, and birds are each called to flourish in our respective habitats, how can we do it in such a way that we do not cancel out each others' blessings?" Invite participants to offer answers to the question.

Imagine the world without fish or birds.

Form two teams. Tell Team 1 to talk about what the world would be like if there were no birds. Tell Team 2 to talk about what the world would be like if there were no fish. Allow about five minutes for discussion, then ask the teams to tell the entire group the highlights of their conversation.

Review highlights of the section titled "Creation Out of Balance." Ask: How do you respond to the information in the report from the Audubon Society? How do you respond to the

45

news about fish populations reported by *National Geographic*? As an additional option, you may choose to find the reports online and project them on a screen or wall using an LCD projector. See the following sites:

> *audubon.org/news/CBID_NYTimes.html*
>
> *ngm.nationalgeographic.com/2007/04/global-fisheries-crisis/montaigne-text/7*

Talk about "Reclaiming Stewardship."

Read aloud the paragraph below from this section, and then invite participants to tell how they respond to the idea.

> I cannot help but wonder what would happen if the Consumer Price Index, a popular indicator of the health of the economy, were re-invented as the Stewardship Price Index. An index such as this could reveal the health of our economy, the health of the planet's underlying ecology, and the health of the poor. By pinpointing the human and ecological costs of our choices in dollars and cents, we might see the real price tag of our lifestyles.

Read aloud the following question from the author: "Is it too late for us to make a difference and to learn to live together in fruitful harmony?" Invite participants to offer answers to the question and to explain their responses.

Read aloud the following expression of hope from the author, and then invite participants to tell whether they agree or disagree and to explain their responses.

> However, as Christians we live by hope, so the answer must be yes. It is not a blithe yes, though, for in order for it to be fulfilled, this yes must be grounded in the Scriptures, sounded out by science, enacted in faith, and lived out in our daily lives. Fortunately, no one is better situated to do this than communities of faith. We have the moral backing. We have the theological framework. We have the organization. We have multigenerational memory to ground us. We have future generations to consider. I am not saying it will be easy. Likely it will not be. However, God's creation is worth our best efforts.

Tell personal stories of "Reclaiming Nature."

Form teams of two or three. Invite the teams to tell one another stories about their experiences in nature. For example, they may have experienced a camping trip like the one described in the book, a day trip, a walk in the park, or just an afternoon sitting in the backyard. Ask them to describe the sights, sounds, and feelings of the experience.

After about five minutes, tell the teams to discuss the following questions: What insight does your experience in nature offer to reclaiming our roles as stewards of God's creation? to living out our identities in the image and likeness of God?

Green Fact

Review the material about incandescent light bulbs and compact fluorescent light bulbs (CFLs) in "Green Fact: CFLs." Ask: Where in your home would you use incandescent bulbs? Where would you use CFLs? What are you currently using in your home?

Spotlight on Science: Global Weirding

Review highlights of the material from NASA in this section. Ask: What weird things have you observed that you think might be attributed to climate change?

Spotlight on Science: What Is Causing Climate Change?

Review highlights of the information in this section. As an additional option, view the websites listed in the footnotes using an LCD projector. Ask: How do you respond to these reports?

Greening the Church

Read the material in this box. Survey your church, and take notes using the checkpoints provided.

Look Ahead

Encourage the group to read Chapter 3, "Reduce," and the Bible readings (Genesis 2:1-3; Exodus 20:8-11; 31:12-17; Leviticus 25; Deuteronomy 5:12-15) before the next session.

Invite participants to contact one another by phone or e-mail to offer mutual support or to talk about what they are doing to be better stewards of creation.

Close the Session

Light the candle on the small table in the center of your group. Lead your group in the following prayer:

Gracious God, you have created us in your own image to bless and care for all that you have made. Help us to reclaim a right relationship with your whole creation that the earth might thrive with the abundance you intended. Open our eyes to the beauty that is around us; and help us to be faithful stewards of all your good gifts, being mindful not only of ourselves but of all your creatures and of those who will come after us. This we ask through Jesus Christ our Savior and Lord, who lives and reigns with you and the Holy Spirit, one God, now and forever. Amen.

Reverend Tim Trippel
Evangelical Lutheran Church of America
Worland, Wyoming

3. Reduce

This session explores the environmentally friendly covenant of sabbath.

Genesis 2:1-3; Exodus 20:8-11; 31:12-17; Leviticus 25; Deuteronomy 5:12-15

Prepare

Read and review session materials.
- Pray for God's guidance as you read and think about the content for this session.
- Read Genesis 2:1-3; Exodus 20:8-11; 31:12-17; Leviticus 25; and Deuteronomy 5:12-15. Write notes about insights and questions that occur to you as you read.
- Read Chapter 3 in the book *Green Church: Reduce, Reuse, Recycle, Rejoice!* Make notes about insights or questions you have. Consider how your group might respond to the material. Write questions you think they might ask.
- Review any websites you might want to show the group.
- Review the Chapter 3 session plan.

Gather supplies.
- Bibles
- Additional copies of the book, if needed
- Nametags
- Large sheets of paper (preferably recycled) or a marker-board and markers
- Masking tape
- 8½" x 11" paper (preferably recycled)
- Pens or pencils
- Unscented candle and matches
- (Optional) Audiovisual equipment such as a computer and an LCD projector for viewing websites

Set up the learning area.

- Chairs. Make sure everyone will have a comfortable place to sit. Arrange chairs in a circle to promote group interaction.
- Table for supplies and a place to work. Participants may need to use a tabletop for writing or other creative activities. Make sure to consider the needs of those who have physical impairments.
- Small table for a worship center. Cover with an attractive cloth. Place the unscented candle and matches on the table.
- (Optional) Screen or wall to project websites with the LCD projector

Welcome Participants

- Arrive early. Pray for all participants and for this Green Church session about the covenant of sabbath.
- Greet participants by name as they arrive. Make sure they have a comfortable place to sit.
- Invite participants to share any insights they gained from doing the activities in the "Greening the Church" section.

Open the Session

- Turn to Chapter 3; and invite someone to read aloud the title, the opening Scripture (Genesis 2:1-3), and the paragraph at the beginning of the chapter. Ask: What feelings or thoughts do you have about the value of being busy?
- Lead the group in this opening prayer: God of rest and renewal, guide us as we explore the blessings of your commandment to remember the sabbath and to keep it holy; in Christ we pray. Amen.

Consider the Question

Read aloud the material titled "Question." Ask participants to choose the answer that best fits their sabbath practices. Then ask: Is sabbath still important today?

Explore the Chapter
Consider God's example.

Read aloud Genesis 2:3. Review highlights of the section titled "God Rested." Ask: How do you respond to the idea that God rested from work? What do you think about God blessing a period of time just as God blessed fish, birds, and humans?

Write "Freedom to Be" on a large sheet of paper or on a markerboard. Invite participants to call out words or phrases that come to them when they hear the phrase *freedom to be*. Write their responses on the paper or markerboard.

Write "Freedom to Be Like God" on another large sheet of paper or on the markerboard. Again, invite participants to call out words or phrases that come to them. Write these responses on the paper or markerboard.

Ask: What insights do you gain from following God's example of rest? What does following God's example say to you about the meaning of being created in God's image and the freedom to be like God? What connections do you see between this freedom and stewardship of creation?

Discuss God's sabbath commandment.

Form three teams. Assign Exodus 20:8-11 to Team 1, Exodus 31:12-17 to Team 2, and Deuteronomy 5:12-15 to Team 3. Each team is to read the assigned Bible reading, discuss the following questions, and then report the highlights of their discussion to the entire group. Ask: What does the law say to do on the sabbath? What insights do you gain about God from this law? about humans? about the creation?

Read aloud the following paragraph from the section titled "God Rested":

51

A friend once told me that if I could not say no to a request, then I could not say yes either. All my yeses were not choices; they were simply knee-jerk reactions to other people's requests. In the same way, if we cannot choose to abstain from work or to refrain from busyness, then all of life is one unending to-do list. Is that the purpose of our lives? Not according to the fourth commandment.

Ask the following questions: How important in your life are to-do lists? How would it feel or what would you think about having an entire day without such a list? How does the fourth commandment offer insights about ways to manage our to-do list-lifestyle?

Invite participants to find a partner. Tell them to talk about what it means to "take a break" from something in their lives. Ask: How can a sabbath day help you take a break? What might happen if you decided to take a break by observing the sabbath?

Read aloud the following sentence from the chapter: "The sacred commission of the seventh day is to be a holy oasis in time in honor of the creation and the Creator." Invite participants to imagine a holy oasis in a typical day. Give markers and paper to everyone. Ask them to sketch or write about a holy oasis they might experience during a normal day. Encourage them to tell about what they have written or drawn.

Talk about "Observing the Sabbath."

Review the material at the opening of the section titled "Observing the Sabbath" that tells about Jewish and Christian ways of observing the sabbath. Read aloud the following paragraph from this section:

That is certainly how it was when Connie and Carlyle were growing up. Lifelong Methodists now in their nineties, this married couple grew up in a time when dancing, playing cards, and going to the movies were forbidden on Sunday. Instead, Sunday was spent worshiping, eating family meals, and being involved in quiet play.

Ask: How are Sundays different today? How do you spend Sundays?

Invite participants to review the author's experience of celebrating Jewish and Christian observances. Ask: How do you respond to the author's description of her personal memories of observing sabbath as a Jew and as a Christian?

Read aloud the following paragraph from this section:

> I came to find that the seemingly restrictive "thou shalt nots" of sabbath made room for expansive "thou shalts." Thou shalt enjoy thy life! Just do it without spending money. Thou shalt relax! Just do it without getting in the car or driving anywhere. Thou shalt enjoy nature! Just do it without taking from it. It is a clever setup, really. As with reality television shows that give you a budget of $250 to remake a room or $15 to feed a family of four, it was the restrictions that inspired creativity.

Write "Thou Shalt Not" on a large sheet of paper or on a markerboard. Invite participants to tell what they think are "thou shalt nots" for the sabbath. Write these on the paper or markerboard. Write "Thou Shalt" on another sheet of paper or on a markerboard. Again, invite participants to tell what they think are "thou shalts" for the sabbath. Write their responses on the paper or markerboard. Ask: What connections do you see between these two lists? How does the "Thou Shalt Not" list make the "Thou Shalt" list possible?

Discuss making work and making rest.

Read aloud the following paragraph in the section titled "Observing the Sabbath."

> "On it, you shall not do any work," the text insistently reminds me. Interestingly, though, one translator renders that passage, "you are not to make any kind of work."[1] I surely know how to make work. Just ask my husband. Every new project I take on makes work for him, and vice versa.

Review highlights of the material in the rest of this section about ways we make work for the planet. Ask: How do you see our human activity making work for our planet?

53

Read aloud the following sentences: "Sabbath helps level the playing field. It makes rest for everyone. It also makes rest for the planet." Invite participants to name specific ways that observing the sabbath makes rest for people and for the planet.

Discuss "Sabbath, Science, and Sustainability."

Review highlights of the information about NASA observations on the sabbath. Ask the following questions to stimulate discussion: What, if anything, surprised you about this NASA information? What does the information say to you about the impact of our way of life on the environment? What does it suggest to you about the value of sabbath?

Give reports of the sabbatical year and the Jubilee year.

Read the opening paragraph in the section titled "The Sabbatical Year." Form two teams. Team 1 will read information about the sabbatical year in Leviticus 25:1-7 and in the section titled "The Sabbatical Year." Team 2 will read information about the Jubilee year in Leviticus 25:8-17 and in the section entitled "The Jubilee Year." Ask each team to prepare a report to give the entire group. After the reports, ask the following questions to stimulate further discussion: What challenges and benefits do you see in observing a sabbatical year and a Jubilee year as described in Leviticus 25? How are such observances "about justice"? What would our world be like if we observed these forms of sabbath?

Identify ways to observe the sabbath.

Review the highlights of the section titled "Revisiting Sabbath." Pose the following questions, and then list the group's responses on a large sheet of paper or on a markerboard. Ask: How realistic are weekly sabbaths? sabbatical years? Jubilee years? What do you think sabbath might look like in our world today? What ideas do you have about observing sabbath in our churches and in our individual lives? How might you observe a mini-sabbath?

Green Fact

Review the material about gasoline and carbon dioxide in "Green Fact: A Sabbath From Driving." Ask: How might you take a sabbath from driving each week? What could you do instead of driving?

Spotlight on Science

Review the material in "Spotlight on Science: The Weekend Effect." Ask: What insights does this scientific information offer you about the value of observing sabbath?

Greening the Church

Read the material in "Greening the Church." Use the information here as a checklist for use of energy in your church.

Look Ahead

Encourage the group to read Chapter 4, "Reuse," and the Bible readings (Matthew 6:19-34; Mark 10:17-25; Luke 3:8-14; 12:13-21; and Acts 2:41-47) before the next session.

Invite participants to contact one another by phone or e-mail to offer support or to talk about what they are doing to be better stewards of creation.

Close the Session

Light the candle on the small table in the center of your group. Lead your group in the following prayer:

Most holy God, Creator of the universe and all that is, show us the way to a holy sabbath. Help us to discover that letting go of the busyness that controls our lives can then lead us to an experience of sacred time. Make this time a gift for all the creation. Grant us vision to see the beauty of the land and its creatures, not as our possession but as your gift. Give us the wisdom to be stewards and protectors of that land. Most of all, allow us to see that living this new way will immerse us into true sabbath. Amen.

Reverend Warren Murphy, Retired
Episcopal Diocese of Wyoming

---

[1] *The Schocken Bible, The Five Books of Moses: Genesis, Exodus, Leviticus, Numbers, Deuteromony, A New Translation With Introduction, Commentary, and Notes,* Volume 1, by Everett Fox (Schocken Books, 1995); page 371.

4. Reuse

This session examines the acquisition and accumulation of "stuff" and the value of reusing things.

Matthew 6:19-34; Mark 10:17-25;
Luke 3:8-14; 12:13-21; Acts 2:41-47

Prepare

Read and review session materials.

- Pray for God's guidance as you read and think about the content for this session.
- Read Matthew 6:19-34; Mark 10:17-25; Luke 3:8-14; 12:13-21; and Acts 2:41-47. Write notes about insights and questions that occur to you as you read.
- Read Chapter 4 in the book *Green Church: Reduce, Reuse, Recycle, Rejoice!* Make notes about insights or questions you have. Consider how your group might respond to the material. Write questions you think they might ask.
- Review any websites you might want to show the group.
- Review the Chapter 4 session plan.

Gather supplies.

- Bibles
- Additional copies of the book, if needed
- Nametags
- Large sheets of paper (preferably recycled) or a markerboard and markers
- Masking tape
- 8½" x 11" paper (preferably recycled)
- Pens or pencils
- Unscented candle and matches
- Hymnals or songbooks that contain the hymns "One

Bread, One Body" and "I Am Your Mother (Earth Prayer)." Lyrics to "One Bread, One Body" can be easily located with an online search. The hymn "I Am Your Mother (Earth Prayer)" is in the songbook *The Faith We Sing*, 2059 (Abingdon Press).

- Two sheets of poster paper
- Several old magazines that contain photos
- Scissors
- Glue
- (Optional) Audiovisual equipment such as a computer and an LCD projector for viewing websites

Set up the learning area.

- Chairs. Make sure everyone will have a comfortable place to sit. Arrange chairs in a circle to promote group interaction.
- Table for supplies and a place to work. Participants may need to use a tabletop for writing or other creative activities. Make sure to consider the needs of those who have physical impairments.
- Small table for a worship center. Cover with an attractive cloth. Place the unscented candle and matches on the table.
- (Optional) Screen or wall to project websites with the LCD projector

Welcome Participants

- Arrive early. Pray for participants and for this Green Church session about the accumulation of "stuff" and the value of reuse.
- Greet participants by name as they arrive. Make sure they have a comfortable place to sit.
- Invite participants to tell about any insights they gained from doing the activities in the "Greening the Church" section.

Open the Session
- Invite someone to read aloud the title, the opening Scripture (Matthew 6:19-21), and the paragraph at the beginning of Chapter 4. Invite the group to spend a few moments in silent, prayerful reflection.
- Lead the group in this opening prayer: God, you never throw us away. You heal us, renew us, transform us, and reuse us day after day. We thank you! Guide us as we consider the value or harm of what we accumulate and how we help our world as we find ways to reuse what we have; in Christ we pray. Amen.

Consider the Question
- Read aloud the material titled "Question." Ask participants to mark the response that best matches their perception of how much "in the world" their congregation might be.

Explore the Chapter
Have a Bible study.

Form four teams. Assign each team one of the following Scripture readings: Matthew 6:19-34; Mark 10:17-25; Luke 3:8-14; 12:13-21; and Acts 2:41-47. Invite the teams to read their assigned Scripture passages aloud and then discuss the following questions: What does the Scripture say to you about the value of accumulating things in our world? What challenges you about the reading? Do you think the Scripture applies easily to our contemporary way of life? Why or why not? What does the reading say to you about reusing what we have? What connections do you see between the reading and the well-being of God's creation? How does the reading inform God's call to us to be good stewards of God's creation?

After about ten minutes, reassemble the teams into one large group. Invite someone from each team to tell about their assigned Scripture reading and about the highlights of their team's responses to the questions.

Discuss attending to the possessions of a loved one.

In the section "Treasures on Earth," read aloud the opening paragraph, which tells about the author and her husband attending to the possessions of family members. Ask: When have you had to take care of the possessions of a loved one? What was the reason for having to take this responsibility? What was it like for you?

Talk about our "stuff."

Review highlights of the section titled "Treasures on Earth." Ask the following questions to stimulate discussion: What is the status of the "stuff" in your household? What kinds of things do you feel you must keep? What kinds of things do you throw away? What feelings or thoughts do you have about your possessions? The author tells us that *store up* and *treasure* come from the same Greek root. Therefore we can accurately say, "Treasure up treasures important to God." How do you respond to this translation? What kinds of treasures do you think are important to God?

Explore hymns.

Form two teams. Assign the hymn "One Bread, One Body" to Team 1 and "I Am Your Mother (Earth Prayer)" to Team 2. Ask them to review the words of their hymn and identify what it says about what we share in common with others. If you have time and if your group likes music, you may choose to sing the hymns. Ask the teams to report the highlights of their discussion with the entire group.

Read aloud the following sentences from the section titled "All Things in Common":

> Going green is ultimately about respecting the well-being of every community on earth, from the smallest organisms within our bodies to the

grandest natural ecosystems, to the families who live in every corner of the earth. . . . Our drive for affluence is depleting the earth and depleting us.

Ask the group: How do you respond to this assertion? Do you agree or disagree? Explain your response.

Make a list of disposables.

Read aloud the following quotation: "Use it up, wear it out, make it do, or do without." Ask: How do you respond to this quotation? Has anyone in your memory said something similar? Who? Do you think people today are as likely to live by this motto as our grandparents or great-grandparents? Why or why not?

Write "Disposable" at the top of a large sheet of paper or on a markerboard for all to see. Invite participants to name aloud the things they use that are disposable. Write these on the paper or the markerboard. Ask: What is the value of these disposable things? What do you see as the consequences of using such disposable things? How might items on the list be reused? What alternatives do you see for disposables on the list?

Discuss Magic Mountain.

Review highlights of the author's experience of life related to the garbage dump in the Philippines called Magic Mountain. Ask: What feelings or thoughts does this story stir up in you? What does the story say to you about what we do with our trash? How does the story speak to the topic of this chapter, which is reuse? Tell the group what this sentence says to you: "Everything goes somewhere."

Write the following questions on a large sheet of paper or on a markerboard: Do I need this? How long will it last? Can it be reused? What will I do with it when I am finished with it? Where will it wind up? What impact will it have on the planet? Invite someone to read the questions aloud. Ask: What might you do differently if you asked yourself these questions each time you purchased something?

Create posters of abundant life and affluent life.

Review highlights of the section titled "Abundance, Affluence, and Happiness." Ask: How do you respond to the assertion by Peter Sawtell that we have confused "life abundant" with "life affluent."

Form two teams. Give each team a sheet of poster paper, several magazines, scissors, and glue or tape. The teams will use the supplies to create posters. Ask Team 1 to create a poster that illustrates abundant life. Ask Team 2 to create a poster that illustrates affluent life. Ask the teams to find pictures in the magazines, cut or tear them out, and tape or glue them to the poster paper to create their posters. When they have finished, invite the teams to tell about their posters.

Ask: What do the posters say to you about the differences and similarities between abundant life and affluent life?

Discuss the benefits of community.

Read aloud the following quotation from the book:

> Studies show that personal connections can stave off death, disease, and divorce. A sense of belonging brings comfort, opportunity, and fellowship; and it is easier on the earth. The more we share, the less the earth has to produce.

To stimulate further discussion, ask: What benefits do you see in being part of a group? How do you see the relationship between community and the well-being of the earth?

Suggest ways to reuse.

Review highlights of the examples of reuse in the section titled "Choose to Reuse." Invite participants to suggest ways to reuse things in the congregation. Write their responses on a large sheet of paper or on a markerboard. Together narrow down the list to two or three items the group thinks could be done by the congregation. Consider taking on one of the ideas as a group project.

Green Fact

Review the information in "Green Fact: Junk Mail." Encourage participants to follow the instructions for reducing the amount of junk mail they receive.

Spotlight on Science

Review the material in "Spotlight on Science: A Floating Garbage Patch." As an additional option, encourage the group to look at the websites listed in the footnotes. Ask: What insights does this scientific information offer you about what we throw away and about the value of reusing things?

Greening the Church

Read the material in "Greening the Church." Use the information as a checklist for ways you might reuse materials in your congregation.

Look Ahead

Encourage the group to read Chapter 5, "Recycle," and the Bible readings (Genesis 2:7-15; 3:19; Psalms 90:1-6; 103:13-18; Ecclesiastes 3:1-2; 1 Corinthians 15:42-55; and 2 Corinthians 5:14-17) before the next session.

Invite participants to contact one another by phone or e-mail to offer mutual support or to talk about what they are doing to be better stewards of creation.

Close the Session

Light the candle on the small table in the center of your group. Lead your group in the following prayer:

To the God of the junk drawer and the linen closet, we meet you with humility. We come to you with questions, with concerns, and with a misguided sense of abundance. How do we relinquish the stranglehold that indifference has placed on our hearts?

How do we differentiate between excess and necessity?

Oh God, give us the strength to recognize our hoarding mentality and the courage to change our careless ways.

We pray for your guidance as we replace our skewed sense of entitlement with a healthy desire for recreation.

For the sake of all creation, please reuse us as a testimony of promise and possibility.

With earnestness we pray. Amen.

> Reverend Hope Hodnett
> Director of Youth Ministries
> Vine Street Christian Church
> (Disciples of Christ)
> Nashville, Tennessee

5. Recycle

This session explores the benefits of recycling, or turning one thing into another, as a practice of biblical stewardship.

Genesis 2:7-15; 3:19; Psalms 90:1-6; 103:13-18; Ecclesiastes 3:1-2; 1 Corinthians 15:42-55; 2 Corinthians 5:14-17

Prepare

Read and review session materials.
- Pray for God's guidance as you read and think about the content for this session.
- Read Genesis 2:7-15; 3:19; Psalms 90:1-6; 103:13-18; Ecclesiastes 3:1-2; 1 Corinthians 15:42-55; and 2 Corinthians 5:14-17. Write notes about insights and questions that occur to you as you read.
- Read Chapter 5 in the book *Green Church: Reduce, Reuse, Recycle, Rejoice!* Make notes about insights or questions you have. Write questions you think they might ask.
- Review any websites you might want to show the group.
- Review the Chapter 5 session plan.

Gather supplies.
- Bibles
- Nametags
- Large sheets of paper (preferably recycled) or a marker-board and markers
- Masking tape
- 8½" x 11" paper (preferably recycled)
- Pens or pencils
- Unscented candle and matches
- A roll of butcher paper and colored markers
- (Optional) Audiovisual equipment such as a computer and an LCD projector for viewing websites

Set up the learning area.

- Chairs. Make sure everyone will have a comfortable place to sit. Arrange chairs in a circle to promote group interaction.
- Table for supplies and a place to work. Participants may need to use a tabletop for writing or other creative activities. Make sure to consider the needs of those who have physical impairments.
- Small table for a worship center. Cover with an attractive cloth. Place the unscented candle and matches on the table.
- (Optional) Screen or wall to project websites with the LCD projector

Welcome Participants

- Arrive early. Pray for all participants and for this Green Church session about recycling.
- Greet participants by name as they arrive. Make sure they have a comfortable place to sit.
- Invite participants to tell about any insights they gained from doing the activities in the "Greening the Church" section.

Open the Session

- Invite someone to read aloud the title, the opening Scripture (Ecclesiastes 3:1-2), and the paragraph at the beginning of the chapter. Invite the group to spend a few moments in silent, prayerful reflection.
- Lead the group in this opening prayer: God of resurrection and renewal, we thank you for the gift of life. Guide us as we look at the cycle of life in your creation. Inspire us and guide us as we explore the value of recycling; in Christ we pray. Amen.

Consider the Question

Read aloud the material titled "Question." Invite participants to rate their recycling habits. If anyone would like to talk about their responses, allow them to do so.

Explore the Chapter

Have a Bible study.

Form three teams. Assign Genesis 2:7-15 and 3:19 to Team 1, Psalm 90:1-6 and 103:13-18 to Team 2, and 1 Corinthians 15:42-55 and 2 Corinthians 5:14-17 to Team 3. Invite the teams to read their assigned Scriptures and discuss the following questions: How does the Scripture reading offer hope? What connections do you see between this Scripture and the concept of recycling? How do you think it offers a biblical foundation for the practice of recycling?

Ask the teams to choose someone to report the highlights of their discussion to the entire group.

Share personal observations of the cycle of life.

Review highlights of the material about gardens in the section "The Cycle of Life." Invite participants to tell about their observations of the cycle of life. If you have time and if weather permits, you may want to take a walk outside. When the walk is finished, invite participants to tell about anything they saw that reminded them of the cycle of life.

Read aloud the following paragraph from "The Cycle of Life":

> Nowhere do we see the cycle of life more powerfully than in the life and death of Jesus. If recycling is transfiguring something old into something new, then resurrection is the ultimate in recycling! One bumper sticker sighted in New York City says, "Resurrection—God's Recycling Plan."

Stimulate discussion by asking the following questions: How do you respond to the author's comparison of recycling and resurrection? Does it make sense to you? Why or why not?

Review and discuss "New Life for Trash."

Review highlights of the section "New Life for Trash." Ask the following questions: In what ways do you think recycling is "holy and wholly biblical"? The author calls throwing away plastic bottles a "national security issue" because plastic is a product made from petroleum. How do you respond to her comment? What thoughts or feelings do you have about recycling as a moneymaking practice that turns trash into cash?

Read aloud the final paragraph in this section about the church in Yakima, Washington. Ask: Do you know stories about other churches that have done something similar? What benefits do you see in a church or other group working together to recycle?

Suggest "upcycling" ideas.

Review highlights of the section "Downcycling, Upcycling, and Resurrection." Ask: What insights do you gain in this section about the ways we recycle? What benefits do you see in upcycling, or turning trash into something new?

Invite participants to suggest ideas about things that might be upcycled to create new commodities or products. List their ideas on a large sheet of paper or a markerboard.

Ask: How do you think upcycling relates to resurrection?

Review and discuss "Green Church."

Tell the group that the section called "Green Church" tells about churches that have built or rebuilt their facilities to reflect the "upcycled resurrection life." Review the examples mentioned. Invite participants to tell about any churches or buildings they know about in which similar things were done.

Create a mural of "One Thing Leads to Another."

Review highlights of the author's story about the effects of her individual choice on a man in her congregation. Remind the group of the questions that started the session: Do you believe the world can be a better place because you choose to recycle? If so, how can it be better?

Invite the group to imagine the effect of an individual choice they might make and how it might lead to another action and thus multiply the benefits of recycling. Ask them to create a group mural on a long strip of butcher paper by encouraging participants to use colored markers to draw or write about what they imagine. When the group is finished, ask participants to tell about what they have written or drawn. Display the mural for all to see.

Green Fact

Review the information in "Green Fact: Recycling." Ask: What surprised you in the list of items and how long they last? How do you respond to the costs associated with methods of dealing with trash?

Spotlight on Science

Review the material in "Spotlight on Science: Close the Loop." Ask: What insights does this scientific information offer you about the economics of recycling? What recycled paper products do you think you might be able to purchase on your next shopping trip?

Greening the Church

Read the material in "Greening the Church." Use the information as a checklist for ways your congregation might recycle.

Look Ahead

Encourage the group to read Chapter 6, "Rejoice!" and the Bible readings (Psalms 19:1-6; 148:7-10; 100:1-5; Isaiah 11:6-9; 35:1-2; 43:18-21; 55:9-13; 65:17-18; Mark 16:15; John 3:16-17; Romans 6:1-4; 8:19-25; 1 Corinthians 15:58; and Revelation 21:1-5) before the next session.

Invite participants to contact one another by phone or e-mail to offer mutual support or to talk about what they are doing to be better stewards of creation.

Close the Session

Light the candle on the small table in the center of your group. Lead your group in the following prayer:

O Holy Creator,
    we thank you for this amazing cycle of life!
We seek your presence throughout our lives.
Help us to look more closely at the cycles of your Earth;
    allow us to learn from Nature,
    and to see birth, growth, death, and resurrection all around us.
Take us from where we are now, to where you want us to be.
Strengthen us as stewards of your creation.
    Help us to see our niche in the larger ecology of life,
    to actively care for ourselves and each other,
    and to make a difference in the world through your Spirit.
In the name of our Lord Jesus we pray,
Amen.

Rev. William R. Morris
Burns Memorial United Methodist Church
Aurora, Colorado

6. Rejoice!

This session explores ways in which rejoicing affirms our faith in God's promises and our role as co-creators with God.

Psalms 19:1-6; 148:7-10; 100:1-5; Isaiah 11:6-9; 35:1-2; 43:18-21; 55:9-13; 65:17-18; Mark 16:15; John 3:16-17; Romans 6:1-4; 8:19-25; 1 Corinthians 15:58; Revelation 21:1-5

Prepare

Read and review session materials.

- Pray for God's guidance as you read and think about the content for this session about rejoicing in God's presence and our roles as co-creators with God.
- Read Psalms 19:1-6; 148:7-10; 100:1-5; Isaiah 11:6-9; 35:1-2; 43:18-21; 55:9-13; 65:17-18; Mark 16:15; John 3:16-17; Romans 6:1-4; 8:19-25; 1 Corinthians 15:58; and Revelation 21:1-5. Write notes about insights and questions that occur to you as you read.
- Read Chapter 6 in the book *Green Church: Reduce, Reuse, Recycle, Rejoice!* Make notes about insights or questions you have. Consider how your group might respond to the material. Write questions you think they might ask.
- Review any websites you might want to show the group.
- Review the Chapter 6 session plan.

Gather supplies.

- Bibles
- Nametags
- Large sheets of paper (preferably recycled) or a marker-board and markers
- Masking tape

- 8½" x 11" paper (preferably recycled)
- Pens or pencils
- Unscented candle and matches
- (Optional) Audiovisual equipment such as a computer and an LCD projector for viewing websites

Set up the learning area.

- Chairs. Make sure everyone will have a comfortable place to sit. Arrange chairs in a circle to promote group interaction.
- Table for supplies and a place to work. Participants may need to use a tabletop for writing or other creative activities. Make sure to consider the needs of those who have physical impairments.
- Small table for a worship center. Cover with an attractive cloth. Place the unscented candle and matches on the table.
- (Optional) Screen or wall to project websites with the LCD projector

Welcome Participants

- Arrive early. Pray for all participants and for this Green Church session.
- Greet participants by name as they arrive. Make sure they have a comfortable place to sit.
- Invite the participants to tell about any insights they gained from doing the activities in the "Greening the Church" section.

Open the Session

- Invite someone to read aloud the title, the opening Scripture (Revelation 21:1-2), and the paragraph at the beginning of the chapter. Invite the group to spend a few moments in silent, prayerful reflection.

• Lead the group in this opening prayer: God of hope and promise, even as we grieve about the harm we have caused to your creation, we know that our actions can make a difference in our world. You are with us, and you are working through us for a new creation. We thank you and praise you; in Christ we pray. Amen.

Consider the Question

Read aloud the material titled "Question." Encourage participants to choose the answer that best describes how they envision life in God's new creation.

Explore the Chapter

Have a Bible study.

Assign the following Scriptures to individual participants in your group: Psalms 19:1-6; 148:7-10; 100:1-5; Isaiah 35:1-2; 55:9-13; 65:17-18; Mark 16:15; John 3:16-17; Romans 6:1-4; 8:19-25; 1 Corinthians 15:58; Revelation 21:1-5. Invite group members to take turns reading the assigned Scriptures aloud to the entire group.

After all the Scriptures have been read aloud, invite the group to be silent for a moment and to reflect upon what stood out for them as they read or heard the Scriptures. Ask the following questions to stimulate discussion: What do the Scriptures say to you about hope? about God's activity? about your actions to become a better steward of God's creation? How or why do these Scriptures inspire people to rejoice?

Tell about favorite places in nature.

Invite participants to tell about the places in nature that mean most to them and why.

Review highlights of the material in the section titled "God Is a Nature Lover." Ask: What particularly stands out for you in this section? How do you respond to the assertion that God loves creation? that God sustains creation? What challenges you about these assertions? How do you see hope in Paul's image of the creation that "waits with eager longing for the revealing of the children of God" (Romans 8:19)?

Explore God's "new thing" in contemporary life.

Read aloud Isaiah 43:18-21 and Revelation 21:5. Review highlights of the material about the author's hike in the section "God Makes All Things New." Invite participants to tell how they see God's "new thing" in our contemporary world. Ask: How does God's "new thing" offer opportunities for rejoicing?

Read aloud Isaiah 11:6-9, the vision of the Peaceable Kingdom. Give everyone paper and pens, pencils, or markers. Invite participants to sketch or write about this vision as it might exist in our contemporary world. Encourage them to tell about what they have drawn or written. Ask: What challenges you about this vision? What gives you hope? How does it invite you to rejoice?

Read aloud the following quote from this section: "If God will one day create a new heaven and new earth, doesn't that let us off the hook when it comes to environmental stewardship?" Ask: What is your response to this question?

Read aloud 1 Corinthians 15:58. Ask: How does this Scripture reading affirm our role in environmental stewardship? How might it give us reason to rejoice? How do you think we participate with God in creating God's "new thing"?

Discuss images of Earth Rise.

(Optional) If possible, project images of *Earth Rise* for all to see. You can locate the images easily by typing the words *Earth Rise* into a search program on your computer. If you do not have access to a computer, the Internet, and an LCD projector, you may be able to find a poster or photo in a bookstore.

Review highlights of the section titled "Earth Rise." Ask whether anyone remembers when the images of Earth as viewed from space were first published. Invite them to tell about their initial responses and what they felt or thought about when they first saw the images. Ask: How does the image of Earth rising invite you to rejoice?

List examples of good stewardship.

Invite someone to read aloud Mark 16:15. Tell participants to review quickly the section titled "Good News to the Whole Creation" and think of examples of good news they have observed or participated in (planting trees, cleaning a river, avoiding the purchase of bottled water, saving a fish). After a few moments, invite the group to give their thoughts. List these on a large sheet of paper or on a markerboard for all to see.

Invite participants to name other actions of good news to the whole creation that they know about. Add their examples to the list. Ask: How does this good news give us reason to rejoice?

Identify opportunities for good stewardship.

Ask the following questions from the section "What About You?" to stimulate ideas for good stewardship: Have you ventured beyond the four walls of your church? Who or what do you see when you do? Do you see concrete or pavement, meadows or mountains, subdivisions or sky? Do you see the homeless or McMansions? Invite participants to tell what they see and offer good stewardship ideas that emerge. Make a list of their ideas. Choose one or two that might work as a group project.

As an additional option, consider whether your church might incorporate the ideas in the companion book to this study, *7 Simple Steps to Green Your Church.*

Green Fact

Review the material about the value of trees in "Green Fact: Plant a Tree." Encourage participants to consider planting a tree.

Spotlight on Science

Review the material in "Spotlight on Science: Your Carbon Footprint." Follow the instructions for neutralizing your carbon footprint.

Greening the Church

Read the material in "Greening the Church." Use the information here as a checklist for ways you might share your joy about caring for God's creation. Plan a worship service that focuses on the stewardship of creation.

Look Ahead

Invite participants to talk about things they have learned that have encouraged an ongoing commitment to be good stewards. Ask: What gives you hope? What worries you? What makes you want to rejoice?

Encourage the group to do the follow-up activities described in the "Greening the Church" section and to continue conversations with those who participated in the group.

Close the Session

Light the candle on the small table in the center of your group. Lead your group in the following prayer:

Rejoice: This is our home!

In You, O God, we pray
   that we may all be one—
      in our hope,
      in our compassion,
      in our joy.

In You, O God, we pray
   that we may all be one
      with those who dance with the Spirit,
      with those who sing for the earth,
and with those who cannot speak for themselves.

In You, O God, we pray
   that we take delight in the world
     You have made.

And, that, *together*
   with those who worry and live in need,
   with those who love and hope and pray,
   with those who swim and crawl and glide . . .
   may we rejoice because . . .
     this is our home.
Amen!

              Reverend Dr. Sally Palmer, Retired
              United Church of Christ
              Laramie, Wyoming